I0608117

Justina Ford
Medical Pioneer

Justina Ford
Medical Pioneer

A NOW YOU KNOW BIO

Joyce B. Lohse

Filter Press, LLC
Palmer Lake, Colorado

To my sister Judy

Library of Congress Cataloging-in-Publication Data

Lohse, Joyce B. (Joyce Burke), 1950-
 Justina Ford, medical pioneer / Joyce B. Lohse.
   p. cm. – (A now you know bio)
 ISBN 0-86541-074-7 (pbk. : alk. paper)
 1. Ford, Justina, 1871-1952–Juvenile literature. 2. African American
women physicians–Colorado–Denver–Biography–Juvenile literature.
I. Title. II. Series.
 R154.F713L64 2004
 618.2'0092–dc22   2004022381

Copyright © 2004 Joyce B. Lohse – All Rights Reserved

Cover photo courtesy Denver Public Library, Western History
Department, Z-8947.

No part of this book may be reproduced or electronically transmitted in
any form whatsoever including packaging of the content in a different
binding, without written permission of the publisher. Contact Filter
Press, LLC at 888.570.2663.

Filter Press, LLC, Palmer Lake, Colorado.

Printed in the United States of America

Contents

Denver Public Library, Western History Collection, Gene W. Carter Manuscripts, #21029

Justina Ford in her teens, long before she became Denver's "Lady Doctor."

Introduction

She always knew what she wanted. She wanted to be a doctor, but she was born with two strikes against her. She was a woman, and she was African American. How could she reach her goal? How would she ever overcome the barriers of race and gender and have a medical career? After all, doctors were men and white. Or were they?

Justina Ford was a bright young lady. She knew that her strength of character would take her a long way toward achieving her goals. She also realized the value of education. From the beginning, she took her studies seriously. When she entered Galesburg High School, she signed up for difficult courses in math and science and learned her lessons well. She studied hard and achieved grades that would allow her to go to college and pursue her goal to become a doctor.

Education was not all it would take. As a black woman, she would have to work harder than other medical students to prove herself a competent doctor. She would be a pioneer in her profession, one of the first in her field, entering an occupation new to black women. The prospect was frightening. What if medical schools would not accept her and hospitals turned her away? What if patients would not use her services? The uncertainty was enough to trouble the strongest of hearts and bravest of souls.

1 Daughter of a Slave

Justina Laurena Warren was born in Knoxville, Illinois on January 22, 1871, only six years after the end of the American Civil War. Knoxville is a small town a few miles east of Galesburg in western Illinois. Justina was very young when her family moved from Knoxville to the larger town of Galesburg where they lived at 534 West Knox Street. Her mother, who was born into slavery in Kentucky, had adopted the slave owners' last name, Brisco or Briscow. The family was listed as **mulatto** in the Knox County census of 1870 and 1880.

Justina was the fourth surviving child of Melissa Brisco Warren. Melissa had previously been married to Ralph Alexander, who died in Missouri. Justina was the only child born to Melissa and her second husband, Pryor Warren. Melissa was widowed a second time when Justina's father died in 1884.

Melissa Warren worked as a nurse to families in Galesburg. Her mother's job must have impressed Justina. As a child, Justina loved to play hospital, but there was a catch. She would play hospital with her friends *only* if she was allowed to be the doctor. Her half-sister and half-brothers, Emma, Ralph, and John Alexander, usually let her have her way.

Young Justina was so interested in doctors and medicine that she made up diseases and then made up medicines to cure them. In an interview with *Negro Digest* magazine in 1950, she said, "I didn't know the names of any medicines, so I had one standard prescription: tobacco pills. I didn't know the names of any sicknesses, so I invented names."

While some little girls played with dolls, Justina enjoyed **dissecting** chickens.

She wanted to know what was inside the chicken. "I remember that I used to like to dress chickens [cut them up to be cooked] for dinner so I could get in there and see what the insides were like."

In addition to her curiosity about living things, Justina wanted to treat the sick. "And I remember that when neighbor folks were ill I liked to tend them. I hope I didn't do them any harm," she said in her good-natured manner as she reflected on her unusual childhood interests.

2 Justina Becomes a Doctor

Justina realized the importance of a good education early on. She attended Galesburg High School, an **integrated** public school, where she studied hard, took challenging courses, and achieved top grades. Listed as "Jessie" Warren in her high school's alumni history, Justina graduated in 1890. Even though she knew she was working against all odds, she was determined to become a doctor. Education was the key to her goal.

After she graduated from high school, Justina met a man from Chicago who could help her achieve her educational goals. They courted and made plans to be married. It is difficult to know if this was part of Justina's plan to help her achieve her educational goals. After all, a move to the big city of Chicago would place her near colleges where she could receive the education needed to become a doctor.

On December 27, 1892, Justina Warren, a month before her twenty-second birthday, married Reverend John L. Ford. He was ten years older than she. The wedding took place in the Second Baptist Church in Galesburg, where Justina's mother was one of the twelve founders. Perhaps her mother was responsible for introducing Justina to the minister from Chicago.

The newlywed couple moved to Chicago where Justina enrolled as a medical student at Hering Medical College. On June 30, 1899, after many years of hard work and persistence, Justina was awarded a degree in medicine. She met all the requirements for a medical license and was given Illinois medical license #16450. Her childhood dream had come true. Now she could practice medicine as a doctor.

The 1900 U.S. Census showed that the Fords lived in a boarding house on State

Street, in the center of the big, busy city.
The Fords did not stay in Chicago long
after 1900. For a year or so, they lived in
Normal, Alabama, in the Deep South.
Justina was probably the first black woman
to work as a doctor in Alabama.

In September 1902, Justina's mother died
suddenly in the Illinois home where she was
employed as a nurse and domestic servant.
She was buried in Linwood Cemetery in
Galesburg. Dates carved on Melissa P.
Warren's headstone show that she was
born in 1831 and died in 1902. Newspaper
articles described her as one of the oldest
and most respected colored people in the
city, and as a kind woman who enjoyed
taking care of others. This trait was carried
on by her physician daughter.

That same year, the Fords moved from
Alabama into a house at 1921 Curtis Street
in Denver, Colorado. At the time the Fords
moved, Denver was still considered "something of a pioneer town," as Justina
described it. Still, Justina felt the people
of Denver had an accepting attitude toward

These photographs of Dr. Ford and her husband, Rev. J. E. Ford, were printed in the Denver Times on May 18, 1903. The article described a community fair to be held at the Zion Baptist Church where Rev. Ford was pastor.

people of all races. After all, five black physicians and a few female physicians were already practicing medicine in the area. The couple would have a new start in a young town where they could be part of a growing city.

Years later, Justina commented on the move to Denver. "I thought it all through before I came. This is just the place I want to practice." Then, in her usual joking manner, "I tell folks I came to Denver in time to help them build Pike's Peak, and it's *almost* the truth."

Know More!

On a map of the United States, find the states where Dr. Ford lived. Denver was her home for fifty years. What changes in the city would she have seen in the years from 1902 to 1952? Hint: Were the streets of Denver paved in 1902? Was there a municipal airport? How tall was the tallest building in Denver in 1902?

3 Overcoming Obstacles

On October 7, 1902, Justina Ford applied for and received a license to practice medicine in the state of Colorado. It came with a warning.

As he collected the five-dollar fee, the **licensing examiner** told Justina, "I feel dishonest taking a fee from you. You've got two strikes against you to begin with. First of all, you're a lady, and second, you're colored." She was not only the first black woman doctor in Denver and the entire state of Colorado, but also one of very few in the entire country.

Justina was not discouraged. Although her main work was delivering babies, many people in Denver needed a doctor who would take care of them in their homes.

Colorado State Archives, #22366

In order to practice medicine in Colorado, Dr. Ford needed a license. Hers was issued in 1902. Notice that the license refers to "he" and "him" only. There was little expectation that a medical license would be issued to a woman.

Patients with tuberculosis and other respiratory diseases who had come to Colorado to breathe the fresh, healing air were sometimes turned away by Denver City and County Hospital, especially if they had no money to pay for hospital services. People of color were turned away whether they could pay or not. Some immigrants chose to be treated at home because they distrusted the hospitals.

When Justina opened her medical practice in Denver, only three people out of one hundred in Arapahoe County were African American. Denver's population in 1900 was 134,000. That means about 3,350 were African American. About 26,000 people living in Denver had been born in foreign countries. Oriental people, especially Chinese, and European minorities such as Italian, German, Greek, Russian, and Irish were not allowed to use the County Hospital either. Twenty years later, in 1920, when the city's population had almost doubled, the number of African American citizens was about 6,075.

Justina herself was not allowed to treat any patients at the Denver hospital when she began working as a doctor. Membership in the Colorado Medical Society was required before she could join the American

Medical Association. Both memberships were required in order for her to work as a doctor in the hospital. This situation could have put her at a disadvantage in a city that already had 457 physicians, but many of Justina's patients could not be treated in the hospital anyway. Of course, Dr. Ford wanted the option of treating patients in the hospital. She knew that racial **discrimination** was one reason her patients were denied care. Justina would help change this injustice. As she later said, "I fought like a tiger against those things." Justina fought discrimination so that she could get the hospital care some of her patients needed. She could do only so much on her own, and some of her patients suffered without hospitalization. Race and gender were very real obstacles for Dr. Ford.

When the Fords bought a house near the **Five Points** neighborhood of Denver, Justina set up her medical office in their home, offering medical services in **obstetrics, gynecology,** and **pediatrics**. Justina was listed in the 1908 **city directory** at the new address on Arapahoe Street. Word spread quickly that she was a doctor who would care for patients and deliver babies no matter the race, color, or financial status of the patient. She even provided free medical service to the people in **migrant camps** near Denver. When she received the phone call or message from a person in need, she hurried to gather up her black medical bag and went to their aid.

Although Dr. Ford wanted **hospital privileges** for her patients and for herself, there were some positive aspects to having a medical practice that took care of patients in their homes. Most doctors would not

Know More!

When Dr. Ford went to her patients' homes, she carried a black leather bag filled with medicines and medical instruments such as a thermometer. Make your own medical bag. Use a shoebox or similar size box. Decide what you would need to have in the bag in order to help an injured or sick person. Draw or collect the items. Prepare a short presentation explaining your choices. Do you have items in your bag that Dr. Ford would not have had?

treat patients in their homes, which allowed Dr. Ford access to patients who needed **house calls**. People from different cultures often preferred, and some even required, that a female doctor attend to childbirths in their homes. This situation worked in Justina's favor because she was one of the few doctors who would make house calls.

Another positive aspect of Dr. Ford's home care was her careful attention to cleanliness that made home births preferable to hospital births. In 1902 when Dr. Ford arrived in Colorado, Denver City and County Hospital did not have a good reputation. There were reports of unsanitary conditions. The hospital was funded by the city, but there was never enough money to make many improvements.

In the 1920s the hospital was still crowded and unclean. Denver citizens and newspaper reporters pressured the city and the hospital administrators to make changes for the better. The name was changed to Denver General Hospital, and the hospital adopted a new policy of taking care of all citizens regardless of race.

Dr. Ford would no longer be denied hospital privileges because of her race or her gender. The changes meant that now all races could be admitted for care. She would sometimes care for her patients in Denver General, but mostly she took care of her patients in their homes as she had done for years. Although she wanted and needed hospital privileges, she soon discovered that time spent at the hospital interfered with her visits to patients who wanted to be treated at home. She worked at Denver General Hospital for a short time before returning to work from her home office. From her home she could stay in close contact with her patients.

During a half-century as a doctor in Denver, Justina Ford delivered more than 7,000 babies, or one baby every three days or so. She was well known for stopping by unexpectedly to check on her pregnant clients, giving them the benefit of her attention and **prenatal** care. Her reputation

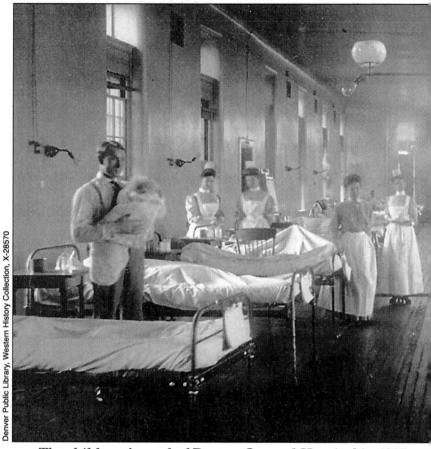

Denver Public Library, Western History Collection, X-28570

The childrens' ward of Denver General Hospital in 1907.

spread all over Denver and beyond. People called her "The Lady Doctor." She treated the needy and disadvantaged of all races: Hispanic, European, Asian, and African American people, as well as Caucasian.

Dr. Ford did not achieve personal wealth or riches through her work as a doctor. Taking care of people was more important

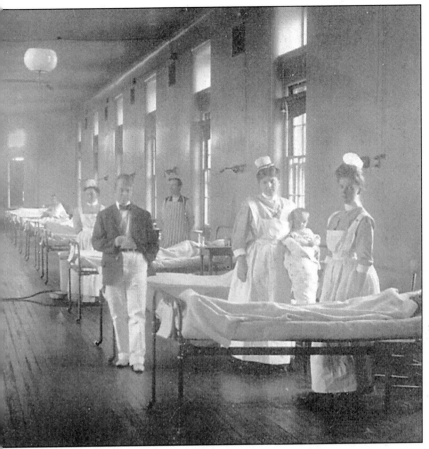

Children of all ages were cared for in one large room regardless of their illness or injury.

to her than money. In the early 1900s, she charged $15 to $20 for prenatal care and delivery. This was a lot of money at the time, and many of her patients did not have money to pay the fee. The unselfish Lady Doctor did not push people to pay their bills, but most found a way to pay. Some patients remembered their debt and paid her years later, even if the "baby" had grown up by then.

If she knew that the patients who paid her had little money, Dr. Ford sometimes bought them groceries with the money they gave her. Those who had no money sometimes paid her with food and gifts. Later, she would quietly donate some of these gifts to charity or to folks who needed them worse than she did. A few items given to her by grateful patients, such as Oriental fabric or hand-woven Mexican blankets, decorated her home.

No one knows how far her generosity went because she did not discuss it, but even the newspaper delivery boy benefited from it. She regularly overpaid him by giving him a silver dollar on collection day. Healthy young people often showed up on her porch, waiting for her to appear. They waited to ask her for financial help with their education. Dr. Ford helped many students of all races achieve their educational goals, even if it meant she had little money leftover for herself.

4 Lady Doctor and Minister's Wife

Strong willed and soft spoken, the small, round woman traveled to her patients by buggy, streetcar, bicycle, or taxi if they could not come to her home office. When she called the taxi company on the phone, she needed only to say her name, and a car was sent to her home. The taxi rushed her to her waiting patient, often at no charge. Some of her patients lived a long distance from midtown Denver. When Dr. Ford arrived for a house call, her authoritative manner made it clear that she was in charge. Good-hearted but firm, she would sit in a rocking chair, calmly sipping tea and giving orders until it was time for the baby to arrive. When the time did come, she removed her outer street clothes and wore a lighter garment to work, so the mother and the new baby would not be exposed to germs brought in on her clothing.

Automobiles appeared on the streets of Denver in the early 1900s, and soon the horse-drawn ambulance was a thing of the past. Dr. Ford eventually bought a car, but she never drove it herself. She never had a driver's license. She hired her nephew to drive her to her patients. When people saw the big, black car passing through the neighborhood, they knew that a new baby was about to be born, and that Dr. Ford was on her way to help.

No one was ever turned away by Dr. Ford because of their gender or race. As she told a *Rocky Mountain News* reporter in 1950, "Folks make an appointment and I wait for them to come or go to see them and whatever color they turn up, that's the color I take them."

Justina spoke at least eight languages or **dialects**. She knew how important it was to communicate with her patients who came from many different countries to work on the railroads and in the mines of Colorado. She avoided confusion in many situations simply by making the effort to learn the languages of her patients.

While Justina took care of her patients, her husband, John Ford, took care of the community's religious needs through his work as minister of the Zion Baptist Church. Reverend Ford was popular with the church members, especially when he stood at the pulpit to preach the gospel. In his first four years at Zion, membership grew from 100 to 400. He was a dynamic leader and shrewd businessman. Under his management as pastor, all of the church's debts were paid. He helped the church increase its treasury by investing successfully in the Golden Chest Mining, Milling and Tunneling Company with other African American investors from the church community. He was vice president of the Golden Chest Mining Company located in Boulder County and served on its board of directors.

Justina's hands were full. In addition to her work as a doctor, she also fulfilled her many duties as the wife of the minister. Her duties were varied and included helping her husband tend to the spiritual needs of the church community and serving as chairperson for the program committee when the church held a fundraising carnival.

Photograph by J.B. Lohse, 2004

Dr. Ford's first husband was pastor of Zion Baptist Church from 1902 until 1907. The church is located at 933 East 24th Avenue in Denver.

The Fords became an important couple in Denver's Five Points neighborhood, as Justina hoped they would. However, in 1907, Reverend Ford became restless to move on to a different church. After many parties and farewell celebrations, Reverend Ford left on a trip to Europe before settling in Jacksonville, Florida, where he was to be minister of Trinity Baptist Church. John and Justina Ford did not share the same plan for the future, and their lives were about to follow different paths.

Perhaps Justina expected her husband to return to Denver after his travels. Members of Zion Baptist Church held Reverend Ford in high regard and hoped that he would return. In the following years, he visited Denver on many occasions to see his friends, his wife, and to preach at local churches. Although he visited often, he never again lived in Colorado.

Justina never lived anywhere else. She did not want to leave her medical practice in Denver. In July 1915, she was divorced from Reverend Ford, who was by then

firmly established in Florida. Although
Justina remained a member of the Zion
Baptist Church, after her divorce she did
not attend services regularly and was less
involved in church activities.

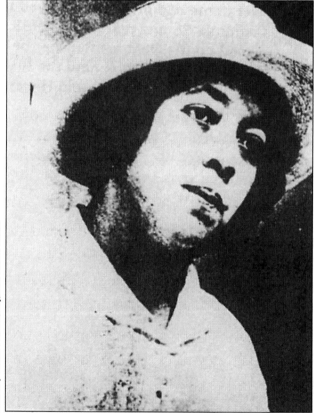

Courtesy Denver Public Library, Ford-Warren Branch

*This undated photograph of young Justina
seems to capture her serious nature.*

5 A Doctor's Life

For a few years, Dr. Ford lived alone. She often had **boarders** living in her house. By 1920, there was a new man in her life. His name was Alfred Allen, and he was eighteen years younger than she. After their marriage, Alf took care of the household and became her chauffeur. He used his skills as a professional woodworker to build bookshelves in her workroom on the second floor of her home.

Justina did not change her last name to Allen. She kept her name as it was written on her medical license and remained Justina Ford, as she had always been known professionally. In her first years of practice, the city directories of Denver listed her as a colored physician.

Eventually, she was listed simply as

> Ford, Justina L. Mrs. Phys.
> 2335 Arapahoe

Life was not easy for the Lady Doctor. Calls from patients came at all hours of the day and night for Justina to tend to childbirth and illness. She slept on a cot by the telephone so she could answer it quickly if it rang in the night. Sometimes, she would go without sleep for days if several patients needed her at the same time.

Her irregular hours required that she take care of herself and maintain healthy habits. There was little time left to care for her nine-room Victorian home.

Alf took care of running the household. He was indispensable. Justina was able to concentrate on her medical work as she made her rounds to take care of patients, knowing that Alf had everything under control at home. They continued to rent out a room or two to boarders, which required extra cooking and upkeep, but brought in needed extra income.

In November 1923, Dr. Ford was involved in a serious auto accident. Alf was driving when the car was hit by a railroad engine used to switch train cars. Justina and Alf recovered from their injuries, but Justina's half-sister, Emma Carter, who was visiting from Galesburg, eventually died from her injuries. It was a sad and difficult time.

Another auto accident in 1931 had less serious consequences. A baseball smashed the windshield of Dr. Ford's car as she and Alf drove past a baseball field at Cathedral High School. She was cut by broken glass but recovered quickly. Alf and Justina may have decided the car was too much trouble. In her later years, Justina often used a taxi to get to her patients.

Dr. Ford developed a habit that served her well during her busy life as a doctor. Each evening, she spent a quiet hour alone reading, writing, studying, praying, or meditating. Quiet time helped refresh her mind and spirit, and contributed to a **spiritual** quality that people often recognized within her. People said her kindness and spirituality showed in her eyes. Nothing came between her and her quiet time routine. If somebody interrupted her, she would firmly ask the person to wait until she finished. She was especially pleased when friends or relatives adopted a quiet time routine into their own lives.

Dr. Ford did not have time for many hobbies or interests outside her practice, but she did enjoy music. In her home, she entertained guests by gathering with them around the piano to sing religious songs.

Although Dr. Ford delivered thousands of babies during her fifty years as a doctor, she had no children of her own. She loved children and delighted in watching the children of friends and relatives, as well as those she had delivered, grow up into adulthood.

Dr. Ford did not receive or expect recognition from Denver's medical community for her work. It was more important that she earn the respect and admiration of the community she served. Although her

Denver Public Library, Western History Collection, Z-8947

*Dr. Ford had no children of her own, but she had
a great interest in the children she treated. In this
photograph she holds one of the 7,000 babies she delivered
during her 50 years of practice.*

manner appeared reserved and coolly professional, her patients knew they could count on her kindness and caring.

Reflecting on her life, Dr. Justina Ford had many happy memories amid the struggles. One story she liked to tell was included in a lengthy *Negro Digest* interview. It told about a little boy who arrived with his mother for her appointment. He wandered all around Dr. Ford's office as though he were looking for something. When Dr. Ford asked what he was looking for, he said, "Where do you keep those babies?" She patiently explained to him that she brought babies to their parents; she wasn't allowed to keep them.

Denver Public Library, Western History Collection, Z-8950

*Dr. Ford in her later years. This photograph
is on display at the Ford-Warren Branch of
the Denver Public Library.*

6 Recognition at Last

As late as 1950, Dr. Justina Ford was the only African American woman doctor in Colorado as she had been for a half a century. In the years after World War II, the soldiers returning from war started families causing a **baby boom**. Although her eyesight was beginning to fail, Dr. Ford was busier than ever.

When she was in her eighties, a friend suggested to Justina that it might be a good idea if she wrote a book about her life and experiences as a doctor for the past half century. Her reply was clear. "A book? Now when would I find time to write a book? I'm getting busier every day."

Times were changing, and so were racial attitudes. On January 3, 1950, Justina was finally allowed to join the Colorado Medical Society, which led to membership in the American Medical Association. This was a huge victory for her, as well as for women of color and future doctors in Colorado. A new door was opened. She still made house calls and worked in her home office by choice, but with the confidence and knowledge that she was allowed to practice medicine in Denver's hospitals.

In 1951, Dr. Ford was honored with a Human Relations Award from the Cosmopolitan Club. The Cosmo Club, as it is still called, began as a social club at the University of Colorado in Boulder. It was a gathering place to encourage intercultural and international understanding. The popular club featured speakers and presentations with international themes, that often addressed racial and ethnic issues.

At one of her final baby deliveries, four months before she died, Dr. Ford made a statement that summed up her philosophy. She was talking with a friend, Petra Lopez-Torres. The two women shared many of the same ideals and viewpoints, including a preference for natural childbirth. After Dr. Ford delivered Ms. Lopez-Torres' seventh child, she speculated about the life of the baby she had just delivered. Dr. Ford said, "This one will be of a generation that will really see opportunity. I won't see the day, you very well may, and this one certainly will...when all the fears, hate, and even some death is over, we will really be brothers as God intended us to be in this land. This I believe. For this, I have worked my whole life." The conversation was part of a 1988 article about Dr. Ford in *Urban Spectrum* and reprinted in *Notable Black American Women, Book II.*

Justina Ford continued treating patients until two weeks before her death. She died in her home on October 14, 1952, at the age of 81. Dr. Ford's funeral was held at Zion Baptist Church, her church home during her many years in Denver. She was buried in Fairmount Cemetery. Justina was survived by her husband, cousins Eugene and Harold Carter, Eva Bradley, Jack

Bradley, Louise Carter, Niece Estella Watkins, two grandnephews, and nine great-grandnephews.

In her **obituary**, *The Denver Star* called her, "A friend of all humanity. Being a doctor, she was also intensely sincere in her desire to preserve all mankind." The newspaper also stated that she was a "Good example for the First Woman Doctor of Color! Great Inspiration!" The headline for the story about the death read, "Pioneer woman doctor struggles and reaches top." This short sentence described her life.

Denver has not forgotten Dr. Ford's many contributions to the people of the city. Her memory has been honored in significant ways. A branch of the Denver Public Library, the Ford-Warren Branch Library at 2825 High Street at 28th Avenue in Denver, was named for her in 1975. In 1987, a group of black health professionals at the University of Colorado Health Sciences Center, organized the Justina Ford Medical Society. The group provided free

health screenings and held medical semi-
nars in the basement of Dr. Ford's house.

Denver residents are fortunate that the
Black American West Museum and Heritage
Center, founded by Paul W. Stewart, pur-
chased the house owned by Justina Ford.
The house was scheduled for demolition
in July 1983 to clear space for parking and
future development. It was saved from the
wrecking ball at the last minute. In 1984,
with help from City Councilman Hiawatha
Davis, a group of concerned citizens
received a $40,000 loan from **Historic
Denver** to move the house about a mile away
in the Five Points neighborhood. The 200-
ton house was painstakingly moved on a
special trailer through the streets of Denver
to its new location. After Paul Stewart and
the board of directors at the Black American
West Museum bought the house, they
received a grant from the City of Denver to
restore the building. Much work was needed
before it could be used as a museum.

Nearly a century after it was built in
1890, the Justina Ford house began its new

life as the Black American West Museum. The grand opening and dedication ceremony took place on September 24, 1988. The beautiful little Victorian home, now located at 3091 California Street, is listed on the National Register of Historic Places.

Courtesy Historic Denver, Inc.'s archival collection

In February 1984, the 200-ton house that once belonged to Dr. Ford was moved through the streets of Denver to its current location on California Street.

Photograph by J.B. Lohse, 2004

In 1988, Dr. Ford's house became the home of the Black American West Museum and Heritage Center. The museum displays show the contributions of African Americans to the development of the West. Visit the museum at 3091 California Street, Denver, Colorado. 303.292.2566.

Visitors to the Black American West Museum and Heritage Center can see displays with photos of Dr. Ford and a reconstruction of her examining room, as well as many exhibits relating to Black American history in Colorado.

In 1989, long after the Colorado Medical Society denied Dr. Ford membership, they named her a "Colorado Medical Pioneer." She was praised by the Society "as an outstanding figure in the development and furtherance of health care in Colorado."

In 1991, students at Manual High School in Denver completed a year-long oral history project honoring Dr. Ford. Individuals whose births had been attended by Dr. Ford were interviewed and told the stories they had heard about her. At the end of the year of study, the students wrote and performed a play entitled, "Ain't No Grave." This combined effort by students, teachers, and performing arts professionals from the black community featured song and dance.

Dr. Ford's memory was again honored when a statue of her was dedicated on June 1, 1998. Sculptor Jess E. DuBois was chosen by the Regional Transportation District Art-at-the-Stations public art program to create a bronze statue of Dr. Ford holding a baby patient. The statue is now located at the 30th and Downing Light Rail train station, across the street from the Black American West Museum.

The Blair-Caldwell Branch of Denver Public Library at 2401 Welton Street was opened in 2003. On the third floor, displays show the history of the Curtis Park and Five Points neighborhoods of Denver, and contributions of Black Americans to Denver's history. A special display honors the work and **humanitarian** efforts of Dr. Ford.

Of course, Dr. Ford would choose as her legacy the people who came into this world as babies she helped deliver. Imagine how she felt when reflecting on bringing more than 7,000 babies into the world. Many of those people and their descendents populate Denver and the Five Points neighborhood.

Photograph by J.B. Lohse, 2004

A bronze statue of Dr. Ford was created by Jess E. DuBois and installed June 1, 1998, across the street from the Black American West Museum and Heritage Center. The museum can be seen in the background.

Always a spirited character, at the advanced age of almost eighty years old, Dr. Ford revealed to *Negro Digest* that she still enjoyed excitement in her life. "Let me tell you about my hobby," she said. "I like to ride ninety miles an hour in an ambulance. That to me is good fun."

Timeline

1871 – Justina Laurena Carter Warren is born in Knoxville, Illinois.

1890 – Justina Warren graduates from Galesburg High School in Illinois.

1892 – Justina Warren [age 21] marries Rev. John Ford in Galesburg, Illinois.

1899 – Justina Ford earns her medical degree in Chicago, Illinois.

1902 – Justina Ford moves to Denver, Colorado.

1907 – Dr. Ford is listed in the Denver City Directory in her new home with medical office.

1915 – Dr. Justina Ford [46] and Rev. John Ford are divorced.

About 1920 – Justina Ford [51] marries Alfred Allen.

About 1925 – Dr. Justina Ford is allowed to practice medicine in Denver's hospitals.

1950 – Dr. Ford joins the Colorado and American Medical Associations.

1951 – Dr. Ford is presented with a Humanitarian Award from the Cosmopolitan Club in Denver.

1952 – Justina Ford [81] dies.

1975 – Ford-Warren Branch of Denver Public Library is named in Dr. Ford's honor.

1988 – Dr. Ford's home is moved to California Street to house the Black American West Museum.

1989 – Colorado Medical Society names Dr. Ford a "Colorado Medical Pioneer."

1998 – Statue of Dr. Ford is installed at a Light Rail Station in Denver.

Glossary

baby boom – significant increase in the population of the United States due to the large number of babies born between 1946 and 1964

boarder – a person who pays for lodging and meals in a private home

city directory – a book published yearly that lists residents and businesses of a city

dialect – a regional variation of language

discrimination – the unfair treatment of a person or group based on differences such as race, gender, or age

dissect – to cut apart or analyze in order to study closer

Five Points – a neighborhood located northeast of downtown Denver. Historically, the center of African American culture in the city.

gynecology – the medical specialty that cares for the reproductive system of women

Historic Denver – non-profit organization that works to preserve the architectural and cultural heritage of Denver, Colorado.

hospital privilege – the right to use medical facilities granted to a physician at the discretion of the hospital

house call – medical treatment and consultation in the patient's home

humanitarian – a person who helps others because of his or her kindness and love of mankind

integrate – to combine different groups, such as blacks and whites educated together in one school

licensing examiner – agent of the state medical board who reviews the qualifications of applicants for medical licenses

migrant camps – a cluster of shelters for temporary workers

mulatto – an individual of mixed black and white ancestry

obituary – a newspaper article that tells about a person's life at the time of their death

obstetrics – medical care during pregnancy through childbirth

pediatrics – medical care of babies and children

prenatal – before birth

spiritual – having to do with the mind, soul, and non-material matters

For Further Study

VISIT: Black American West Museum and Heritage Center, 3091 California St., Denver, Colorado.

VISIT: Blair-Caldwell Branch, Denver Public Library, 2401 Welton St., Denver, 3rd Floor, Western Legacies Museum and Exhibit Space.

READ: Cox, Clinton, *African American Healers*, John Wiley, New York, NY, 2000.

READ: Shikes, Robert H., M.D., *Rocky Mountain Medicine: Doctors, Drugs, and Disease in Early Colorado*, Johnson Books, Boulder, Colorado, 1986.

Bibliography

Alumni, The, High School, 1861-1911, Galesburg, Illinois.

Black American West Museum and Heritage Center (brochure), Denver, Colorado.

Carter, Gene W., Archival Papers (MSS), Denver Public Library, MS-ARL 104.

City Directories, Denver, Colorado, 1915-1935.

Colorado Medicine, "Dr. Justina Ford Honored as First Black Female Physician in Colorado", February 15, 1989, p. 60.

Cox, Clinton, *African American Healers*, John Wiley, New York, NY, 2000.

Daily Register-Mail, Galesburg, Illinois, October 15, 1952, p. 27.

Daily Republican-Register, Galesburg, Illinois, September 26, 1902, p. 1.

Daily Republican-Register, Galesburg, Illinois, August 7, 1993, p. A-3.

Daily Republican-Register, Galesburg, Illinois, March 22, 1998, p. A-7.

Denver Post, Denver, Colorado, October 14, 1952, p. 33.

Denver Post, Denver, Colorado, April 22, 1975, p. 39.

Denver Post (online), Denver, Colorado, May 11, 1991, p. 1E.

Denver Star, Denver, Colorado, October 18, 1952, p. 1.

Dr. Justina L. Ford House, Grand Opening and Dedication Ceremony, program and letter, Denver, Colorado, 1988.

Fairmount Cemetery (booklet), *Distinguished Colorado Women Walking Tour*, Denver, Colorado, 1997, item #11.

Galesburg Weekly Mail, Galesburg, Illinois, October 2, 1902.

Harris, Mark, "The Forty Years of Justina Ford," *Negro Digest*, March, 1950, pp. 42-45.

Hine, Darlene Clark, ed., *Black Women in America: An Historical Encyclopedia*, Vol. 1, Carlson Publishing, NY, 1993.

Historic Denver, Denver, Colorado, December 1983.

Historic Denver, Denver, Colorado, July 1986, p. 6.

Johnson, Connie, "Dr. Justina Ford: Preserving the Legacy," *Odyssey West*, March/April 1988(?), pp. 4-5.

Knox County, IL, Clerk, Marriage License, John E. Ford and Justina L. Warren.

Mauck, Laura M., *Five Points Neighborhood of Denver*, Arcadia Publishing, Charleston, SC, 2001.

Opalanga [Pugh], *She-Roes, Living Her Story* (J-cassette), Olukano Publications, Denver, Colorado, 1990.

Pigford, Clementine Washington, *They Came to Colorado With the Dust of Slavery on Their Backs*, 9 volumes (draft), Denver, Colorado, 1999.

Register-Mail (Daily), Galesburg, Illinois, October 15, 1952, p. 27.

Register-Mail, Galesburg, Illinois, August 7, 1993, p. A-2, A-3.

Register-Mail, Galesburg, Illinois, March 22, 1998, p. A-7.

Rocky Mountain News, Denver, Colorado, October 15, 1952, p. 68.

Rocky Mountain News, Denver, Colorado, April 22, 1975, p. 39.

Rocky Mountain News, Denver, Colorado, February 21, 1982, p. 10.

Rocky Mountain News, Denver, Colorado, July 19, 1983, p. 10.

Rocky Mountain News, Denver, Colorado, February 8, 1984, p. 142.

Rocky Mountain News, Denver, Colorado, June 13, 1989, p. 10.

Rocky Mountain News, Denver, Colorado, February 22, 1991, p. 67.

Shikes, Robert H., M.D., *Rocky Mountain Medicine: Doctors, Drugs, and Disease in Early Colorado*, Johnson Books, Boulder, Colorado, 1986.

Smith, Jessie Carney, *Notable Black American Women, Book II*, Gale Research, Detroit, MI 1996, pp. 229-231.

U.S. Census, 1870, Knoxville, Knox County, Illinois.

U.S. Census, 1900, Chicago, Cook County, Illinois.

U.S. Census, 1910, 1920, Denver, Arapahoe County, Colorado.

Varnell, Jeanne, *Women of Consequence, The Colorado Women's Hall of Fame*, Johnson Books, Boulder, Colorado, 1999, pp. 78-81.

World Book Multimedia Encyclopedia (CD), 1999

Websites

African American Registry:
http://www.aaregistry.com/african_american_history/1506/Justina_Ford_doctor_and_humanitarian

Black American West Museum and Heritage Center:
http://www.blackamericanwest.org/househistory.html

Dr. Colorado's Denver Characters:
http://www.denvergov.org/AboutDenverhistory_char_justinaford.asp

Early Illinois Women:
http://www.alliancelibrarysystem.com/IllinoisWomen/files/MI/htm1MI000008.cfn

History of Cosmopolitan Club at CU:
http://www.plan.cs.colorado.edu/cosmo/history.php

Profiles In Black:
http://www.theblackmarket.com/ProfilesInBlack/BAWMH.htm

Index

Photographs in bold

Acknowledgments

This book would not have been written without the generous help of the librarians, teachers, and staffs of Colorado State Archives, Historic Denver, Fairmount Cemetery, Homestead Elementary School, Zion Baptist Church, Galesburg (IL) Public Library, Knox County (IL) Genealogical Society, Back American West Museum, Koelbel Library, and Denver Public Library Western History Department, Blair-Caldwell Branch and Ford-Warren Branch. Their commitment to preserving and sharing the stories of Colorado's colorful and brave pioneers is our pathway to the past. Thank you to my husband, Don, for making it possible for me to live my dream. Thank you to publishers Doris and Tom Baker for your faith in my work and for allowing me to share your vision.

About the Author

Award-winning author, Joyce B. Lohse, grew up in Illinois where she sometimes spent her school recess time writing stories and poems. She is the author of a dual biography of Colorado's first governor and his wife entitled, *First Governor, First Lady: John and Eliza Routt of Colorado*. She is happiest when researching and writing about the women of the West. Learn more at www.lohseworks.com.